AMONG DREAMS

Other titles by Barry Casselman:

The Rippling Water Sleeve and Other Poems (1969)
Equilibrium Fingers (1977)*
Language, A Magical Enterprise, The Body (1978)
Language Is Not Words (1980)

*Kraken Press

AMONG DREAMS

Stories

Barry Casselman

Kraken Press | Minneapolis | 1985

Copyright © 1985 by Barry Casselman.
All rights reserved.
No part of this book may be performed, recorded or otherwise transmitted without the written consent of the author.

Acknowledgements

"A Huge Living Thing" was first published in *Suplemento Literario do Minas Gerais* (Brazil, 1972), translated into Portuguese by Sergio Sant'Anna.

Kraken Press acknowledges grants from H.B. Fuller Foundation and Savran's Bookstores for the publication of this book.

First Printing — Winter, 1985

Manufactured in the United States of America.

First Edition

ISBN 0-936623-00-4

Cover Design by Steven Sikora
Camera-ready production by Red Sky Typesetting & Graphics

KRAKEN PRESS
3035 17th Ave. S.
Minneapolis, MN 55407

for my parents

Publisher's Notes | 9

Prelude | 11

SKIN | 15

A HUGE LIVING THING | 23

THE BUSINESSMAN | 37
WHO DISAPPEARED

PUBLISHER'S NOTES

The three stories published in this book were written more than ten years ago, and one of them, "A Huge Living Thing," was translated into Portuguese, and published in Brazil even before it was published in English in the United States. Ten years after that publication, Barry Casselman began his collaborations with the American composer Randall Davidson as they prepared a theater performance work which they named *Among Dreams*. "A Huge Living Thing" became the centerpiece of that presentation of three Casselman stories — "Skin" preceding it, "The Businessman Who Disappeared" following it — in which these three enigmatic tales were told by a storyteller in a darkly-lit tent with musicians outside playing accompanying music on conventional and unconventional instruments, and a short-wave radio.

The premiere performance took place on August 10, 1984 at the Union Depot in St. Paul as part of the New Works/St. Paul festival. James Stowell, who had been one of the major forces of experimental theater in the Twin Cities for more than a decade as actor, director and playwright, performed as the Storyteller. The music was played by the *sfz* Ensemble, the resident new music ensemble of the MacPhail Center for the Arts, conducted by Lee Humphries, the ensemble's artistic director. All four performances played to capacity and standing-room-only audiences.

The following year, the "A Huge Living Thing" segment of *Among Dreams* was chosen to be included in the initial program performed by the St. Donat's Music Ensemble of Wales in their first North American tour. It was presented on November 5, 1985 at the University of Minnesota Student Center as part of the British Minnesota Festival with John Rath, who had previously played Escamillo in both the European stage and film versions of Peter Brook's *Carmen*, performing as the Storyteller, and with Wyn Davies conducting. The environment of a tent was created for this performance by seating the audience on the stage with a closed curtain, and even though the resulting seating was twice the capacity available at the premiere, an overflow crowd had to be seated in the theater seats outside the tent.

A revival of the original production of *Among Dreams* with James Stowell, Lee Humphries and most of the musicians from the first performance, was set to open on December 16, 1985 at the Actors Theater of St. Paul as part of its premiere season in its new theater space in downtown St. Paul.

PRELUDE

In early 1982, I walked into Barry Casselman's office. I did not know then that he and I would become collaborators, colleagues, and close friends.

Shortly after talking to him that first time, I read a book of his poems and two short stories he had written. The two stories caught my attention immediately as having the great power and vividness I appreciate most in fiction.

I then approached Barry with the idea of using his texts for an evening entertainment that I was developing. That work, Among Dreams, *was eventually premiered in St. Paul in 1984.*

We chose three stories for Among Dreams, *and they are the stories that make up this book. It seems to me that "Skin," "A Huge Living Thing," and "The Businessman Who Disappeared," like all of Barry Casselman's work, are legs of a journey that unfold in unexpected ways.*

If, as one reads this book, the reader begins to hear music, I won't be surprised. I found that writing music to these words and stories was just a matter of listening, carefully.

Randall Davidson
December, 1985

SKIN

The gentleman returned to his *pension* at nine o'clock, and went directly to the dining room where supper was being served. Some of the diners already there were watching a soccer match on the television that was placed in one corner of the room. The gentleman shared his table with a middle-aged spinster who made strange eyes at him much of the time, though they seldom spoke to each other, and she paid no attention to the television at all. Good evening, he said, and good evening, she said. The salad was already on his plate, and he began to peel off the rind from the sausage slices arranged over the lettuce. He then picked up a black olive, fastidiously keeping his fingers out of the oil, and placed it into his mouth. He put the pit into an ashtray. The waitress, who was also the daughter of the owner of the *pension*, then smiled at him, but she was impatient to put the fish course on his plate so that she could return to the kitchen and prepare for the next serving. Thank you, he said. He looked quickly at the newspaper he had purchased in the street, and he then put it on the floor next to his chair because he did not want to be rude to the spinster. He took some bread from a small basket. It was at least three days old, and quite hard. He squeezed a lemon section over the fish. It had been fried in garlic. Carefully, he cut the fish flesh away from the bones, looking up now and then at the spinster eating her fish. Someone scored a goal, and there was a great commotion in the room, some loud shouts and considerable emotion, but it was difficult for him to determine which side had scored, since he had not been paying attention to the match, for there were boarders here from the west and the south and the capital, as well as from this region. The gentleman did not attempt to interest himself in the game, but went on eating his fish until he had finished with it. Occasionally, he looked up at the color photographs of boats which hung in plain wood frames on one wall. Once again, the young girl came, took away his plate, and replaced it with another. This included a thin, well-done beefsteak and a portion of stewed tomatoes. He poured some red wine into his glass from a green bottle which had no label. He took some more bread, and ate everything hungrily. For dessert, he peeled a banana which had a large, soft brown spot. After this, he excused himself from the table, and nodded to the others (all of whom expected anyone departing from the room to make some gesture), and went to his own room. This space was large, and always seemed cold. There was no heating in the building, and the local populace boasted about this, saying there was no need for furnaces in this climate during the winter, which at its worst was so mild. Besides, each room was provided with warm blankets. The furniture in the room was made of wood, except for the bed which was made of iron, and the bed-table which had a marble top. The walls were dully green. His books were neatly arranged on a shelf he had made by placing two chairs together against a wall. Every afternoon he went to the open-air book stalls, and browsed for novels or whatever other old books he could find. Today, he had purchased nothing. There was a sink near the window, a small towel rack at the side of the sink, and a small glass rack for cups and toilet articles above that. He read his newspaper thoroughly. Then he brushed his teeth and washed his hands. He walked over to the bed and sat down. He took off his socks. He looked at his feet, and put his forefinger between the toes of the right one. He felt some moist black thread fuzz which had come from his socks. He brushed it away. He scrutinized the bottoms of his feet. He took his nailcutter from a brown leather case on the bedtable and began to make small incisions on the ball of one foot. Grabbing the small tags which resulted, he began peeling the skin from the sole back to the heel in narrow strips. The heel itself was more difficult because the skin there came off crossways, but he took care of that. When he had finished with one foot, he turned to the other and completed the same steps. He then went to the small sink at the other side of the room and filled a porcelain bowl with hot water, at least as hot as the *pension* provided, and brought it back to the bedtable. He turned on the bedlamp and sat down again, and began rubbing the water on the tops of his feet. He rubbed until the skin came off in little balls. It was easiest where the skin was hardest. He returned to the sink and took his razor from a box. He then removed his trousers, his shirt, his undershorts and his t-shirt. He also removed his watch. He went back again to the sink, and got a bar of soap and a large towel. Sitting on his bed moments later, he soaked his legs with warm water from the bowl, soaped them, and shaved off the hair. He did the same at his groin, continuing up to his chest (though there was little hair on it) and his arm pits. He remembered the hair between his nates, and went over to the mahogany wardrobe, which had a vertical mirror, and stood with his back to the mirror while using the razor. Finally, he took a scissors from the second drawer of the bedtable and began cutting off his head hair until it was very short. When he had done that, he soaped his head and removed the stubble with the razor. He noticed that he had some fine hairs on his arms, so he went to the sink (the water bowl was now empty) and soaped them and shaved them. He removed the blade from the razor and returned to the bed. Sitting down, he drew one leg up to the edge of the mattress and began cutting into the skin around the ankle, but not deep enough to draw blood. He cut a complete circle. He did the same with the other leg. Then he began peeling the skin in long strips toward the knee. When he had finished with both legs, he removed the skin from his knees as he had done with the tops of his feet, rubbing until the skin came off in balls. This time, however, the balls of skin were white instead of gray — because the soaping had made his skin quite clean. He took the blade again, and cut circles just above the knees, then peeled off the skin to his groin and to the top of his buttocks. This took some time because he could not see clearly the skin on his back. There was by now a considerable quantity of skin lying about, so he stopped for a while and arranged the bits and strips, curling and hardening, into a pile at the center of his bedspread. Then he examined his genitals, and noticed that he had neglected the hair on his scrotum. He went to the sink, took some hot water and soap, lathered the hanging sac, and shaved off the hair. When all the hair had been removed, he changed the angle of the blade in the razor to the sharpest degree, and continued scraping carefully until the skin came off. He took the blade out of the razor, and cut a circle with it at the base of his sex. This he peeled in strips to the glans. At the glans, he cut another circle, and removed its skin very gently and slowly. He then turned his attention to his upper body, and incised a semi-circle around his hips. He removed the skin on his chest and stomach. It did not come off in strips, but in irregularly-shaped sheets. He went over to the mirror again, and with his back to it, cut the skin at the top of his buttocks. Peeling the skin from his back took quite a bit of time, and there were some areas on his back he could reach only after considerable contortion. He also found himself repeatedly moving his hand in the wrong direction when looking in the mirror. After he finished with this, he made two circular cuts at the tops of his arms, and then took off the skin to his wrists. He made a circle cut at the base of his neck, but changed his mind, and removed the skin in this area by hard rubbing. His facial skin came off easily, using the razor, but he took special care around his eyes. The ears were difficult, and took much time. He used the razor as a scraper on the top of his head. He let his lips dry for a few minutes, then peeled them with his fingers. The only remaining skin was now on his hands, but he did not immediately turn to them. Instead, he moved the bedlamp on to the bed, and carefully examined his body for skin that he might have missed. He went to the mirror and looked at his back. He removed bits of skin with the blade. At last, he looked at his hands. He cut circles at the wrists, and peeled off the skin in strips to his fingers. He did the same with his fingers, except for their tips. The skin on his fingertips he bit off with his teeth. The skin along the sides of his fingernails was peeled by hand. He took his fingernail cutter, and trimmed the nails of his fingers and toes, cutting them very short. He put these clippings in a pile that was separate from the pile of skin. He threw away the bits of nails into a wooden wastebasket near his desk. He drew out a large manila envelope from one of the desk drawers, went to the bed, and placed all of the pieces of skin into it, sealed it, and put it under the mattress. He was bleeding only in occasional places; none of it had been intentional. (Sometimes the skin just peeled badly.) He went to his desk and took up the bottle of carbonated lemonade he kept there, and purchased every few days at the small grocery store on the first floor of the building. He opened the bottle, walked over to the sink, picked up a glass (which he washed out with hot water), poured some lemonade into it, and drank. He replaced the bottle on the desk, turned out the lights, pulled the spread off the bed, opened the covers, and climbed in. He went to sleep at once.

A HUGE LIVING THING

One day a huge living thing lifted itself from the Mississippi River in Minneapolis, Minnesota. It rose from a large pool above St. Anthony Falls, which is located under a billboard of the Northern States Power Company. The Northern States Power Company obtains electricity from St. Anthony Falls, but it is only a minor source of power because the utility has built a nuclear power plant in Monticello about thirty miles away.

The large pool above St. Anthony Falls is a few yards below the Central Avenue Bridge which crosses the river at the edge of the business district on one bank, and the edge of the university district on the other. Many persons, while walking across this bridge, have looked down at the pool over the years and noticed, if they looked carefully, what seemed to be a shallow part, an underwater mound of earth or a sandbar. It had always seemed to be there, and was especially noticeable in the sunlight. But it was not a mound or a sandbar. It was a huge living thing.

It cannot be described as any kind of monster, either. Perhaps it might be thought that the very idea of a huge living thing rising from the river in the middle of a city would be a horrible experience, and frightening to children, their parents, and dogs. But the huge living thing which lifted itself from the Mississippi River in Minneapolis, Minnesota, was no dragon or sea lizard or hairy cyclops dripping with algae. Only a few persons saw it come out of the river — some passers-by, a black man fishing from the east river bank, a bus driver and two of his passengers — there were not as many persons in the area as might be supposed because it was a weekend afternoon filled with sunlight. At a time like this, most Minneapolitans leave the city proper and go into the adjacent landscape, a landscape remarkably autographed with thousands of small and medium-sized lakes by a receding glacier centuries before.

No one has satisfactorily explained why the huge living thing came out of the water when it did, although a great deal of investigation followed the incident. The only possible link which was uncovered, and admittedly it is extremely remote, was that at about the same time the huge living thing appeared, a waitress in a Japanese restaurant which overlooks the Falls and the river, opened a window. Normally, this window is never opened because the restaurant is air-conditioned, but the air-conditioning was not working properly that day. While she was clearing the tables from luncheon (the last diners having just departed), a lit cigar someone had left in a wet saucer began to smoke blackly. So she opened, after some effort, one of the windows. Simultaneously, as she was opening the window, the restaurant's proprietor, who was half-Chinese and half-Japanese, turned up the volume of the tape recorder which plays a selection of rare Japanese folk melodies as background music for the dining guests. The proprietor always turned up the volume when the diners left because he loved to hear the music more clearly.

The compositions on the tape that afternoon have been listened to by musicologists, and described by them as extraordinarily evocative while, at the same time, calming — but this proves nothing, and it remains a mystery just why the huge living thing decided to come up when it did.

The sudden appearance of a huge living thing in a civilized city is, as can be imagined, a sensational occurence. This huge living thing, whose appearance was not at all frightening, was somehow familiar. That is, it had a recognizable aspect. Not only that, it spoke words. It spoke only Portuguese words, however. Most persons would agree that this is a very beautiful-sounding language, but it was hardly logical for Minneapolis, Minnesota, with its Scandinavian, German and American Indian heritages. And although the huge living thing spoke only Portuguese — a rich, haunting, sibilant Portuguese — it did not appear to understand any Portuguese spoken to it. It did not matter what dialect or accent was tried; it was no use even repeating the same words it itself had just uttered.

What the huge living thing did appear to understand was Russian. Not the pure Great Russian spoken in Moscow or Rostov-on-the-Don, but a dialect spoken in the Ukraine which was not pure Ukrainian either, although Ukrainian is a distinct Slavic language and spoken by millions of persons.

The bright sunlight days in Minnesota are almost cloudless, and everything seems in the sun's sight. The land in this mesh of freshwater pools is covered with forests and swaying hills which indent the horizon at provocative angles. In this light, someone might think that Minneapolis was a port on the Mediterranean Sea or on the South American coast, but its latitude is much closer to Hudson Bay than to Barcelona or Rio de Janeiro.

When the huge living thing appeared, the citizens of Minneapolis began to assemble on the bridge and on the river banks. The first to stand beside the original witnesses were the residents of the nearby neighborhoods. Not many came from the business district, which was typically deserted on the weekend, but many young persons came from a region known as Seven Corners, a neighborhood of transients, students, panhandlers, teen-age runaways, and young restless couples. Many sculptors, actors, dancers, painters, musicians and writers live there, too, and such persons, for reasons no one has yet explained in a satisfactory way, seem to have special antennae for extraordinary events. They came to St. Anthony Falls as if called by a secret radio transmitter.

Across the river from Seven Corners is the university and its very large campus. Even during the summer, thousands of students go to classes there. Next to this district, the neighborhoods of the poor begin and stretch into the north side of the city like soiled fingers. In these neighborhoods live the American Indians, the blacks and chicanos. They, too, sensed the unusual, and came from the opposite direction of the city to see what was happening.

It took some time for word to spread to the suburbs where the middle classes and the wealthy live. At first, the television and radio stations refused to broadcast news of the event because they did not want to lose their licenses for scaring people with false alarms. This further delayed the news reaching the outskirts of the city. It also so happened that a telephone strike was taking place, part of a national telephone strike that had lasted for fifteen weeks. Most of the telephone equipment, of course, was automated, but by the tenth week the mechanized system had begun to break down without proper maintenance. In Minneapolis and St. Paul, its adjoining city, large areas were temporarily without telephone service for periods of eighteen hours or more on the day when the huge living thing appeared, and this further delayed the news to the outskirts of the city where the middle classes and the wealthy live.

But eventually the news reached them, too, and they rushed in their cars to the excellent expressway system the city has. Even a well-designed road system has a threshhold of efficiency, however, and because twice as many persons live in the suburbs than live in the center city, it was not long before the roads and expressways were choked with cars. Human beings, of course, are very curious — even the middle classes and the wealthy — and this was no everyday happening, but a miraculous event (or what is called a miraculous event); so the drivers and their passengers abandoned their vehicles (most of them were careful to lock their cars before leaving them), and made their way to the Mississippi on foot.

When they arrived at the site of the huge living thing, or as near to that location as they could inasmuch as hundreds of thousands of persons were now assembling there, they beheld the unexpected arrival. The crowd was not tense because the huge living thing made no threatening gestures. On the other hand, the crowd was puzzled because it did not understand the lovely-sounding yet incomprehensible words the huge living thing was uttering.

It so happened that there were a small number of persons in Minneapolis who spoke Portuguese — a few college professors, a handful of foreign students from Portugal and Brazil, several college students who were advanced in their Portuguese studies, less than twenty families who had recently emigrated from Brazil, and a computer salesman who was his company's representative in South America. Roughly the same number of persons spoke the Ukrainian dialect of Russian. Most of these persons had been refugees from the war in Europe.

Eye-witnesses who understood Portuguese reported that while the words the huge living thing spoke were clearly recognizable words, none of them combined in sentences or phrases that were comprehensible. Eye-witnesses who spoke the Ukrainian dialect of Russian, and there happened to be a Ukrainian Orthodox Church just three blocks away, reported that when they spoke to the huge living thing, it would make a gesture indicating that it was listening to them and seemed to understand them (this phenomenon was first noticed when the priest from the church first came to the river bank and was exclaiming loudly in the Ukrainian dialect after seeing the huge living thing). But because they didn't understand Portuguese, and it may not have mattered if they did, they could not establish any verifiable communication between themselves and the huge living thing.

It was only a matter of time before all the Portuguese-speaking and all the Ukrainian-dialect-of-Russian-speaking individuals, at least those who were not confined to their beds, were assembled at a site on the bridge as close to the huge living thing as possible. The problem arose that the mayor and the chief of police and the president of the university and the Ukrainian Orthodox priest and the Portuguese-speaking computer salesman and the governor of Minnesota (who had been flown in from St. Paul by helicopter) could not at first agree on a strategy for communicating with the huge living thing. The only decision that had been made had not been made by anyone in this group, but had come from Washington. The authorities in Washington had decided to seal off the Minneapolis-St. Paul area, and to withhold military intervention until there was some clear and present danger. The governor had called up the National Guard, but these troops waited in buses parked four blocks from the Central Avenue Bridge because it had been apparent from the beginning that there was no immediate threat to life and limb. And the National Guard commander was taking no chances, and would not let his men mingle with the vast crowd.

The assemblage was too amazed to be bored, although nothing particularly dramatic was happening, but it was not the kind of amazement that paralyzes a person. Rather, it was a kind of awe which provokes an inner excitement, and after a time a mood ran through the crowd, especially among the blacks and the chicanos and the American Indians (perhaps because they are closer to magic, or perhaps they are more open to the unexpected), which can only be usefully described by its outward signs, that is, smiles, laughter, gestures of physical contact, occasional contemplative looks, and the like. Studies made afterwards, for whatever they are worth, indicate no common description of the internal aspect of this mood. It appears to have been very idiosyncratic.

As evening approached, the city officials began to worry. Nearly two million persons had gathered along the river. There were no adequate facilities for this throng. When they became hungry enough, they would probably go home, but in the meantime, children and adults, too, were urinating in the river, in backyards, behind trees, even in the open. A horde of food vendors had appeared, as if from nowhere, and

This man had been born in Kozelets near Bobrovits, which are villages near the city of Kiev in the Ukraine. During the war, he had passed some time in Dachau, but had somehow escaped and went, via Peripignan in France, to Barcelona — and from there to Lisbon where he waited out the war. After the war, he had come to New York City, but that city, he came to feel, had become poisoned by whatever was poisoning large cities everywhere. So he moved to Minnesota, in the interior of the country where there seemed to be a biomagnetic pole, tentative and vibrating, that drew him.

This man walked up to the governor, whom he recognized from his photographs in the newspapers, and asked him if he might speak to the huge living thing, explaining that he spoke both Portuguese and the Ukrainian dialect of Russian. He had an intuition, he said, about how to speak to this huge living thing which had arisen so unexpectedly from the Mississippi River in Minneapolis, Minnesota, that afternoon.

The man was pushed and shoved by the small mob on the bridge. The mayor, who had been sitting at the Ukrainian Orthodox priest's feet like a disciple repeating strange-sounding words as if they were some kind of revelation, bounded away from the priest and ran to the governor, threatening to throw him bodily into the river if he didn't let the man speak to the huge living thing. The nearby crowd cheered at this — although it was not clear if they were cheering for the mayor, the governor, or the man. Suddenly, it seemed that the bridge railing might break, and that the man might fall into the river, but the railing held, and when the crowd was persuaded to move back a little, the man was handed an electric megaphone.

He spoke to the huge living thing in a friendly,

strong voice, and with a spontaneous mixture of languages, not just Portuguese and the Ukrainian dialect of Russian. Here is a translation, insofar as it is possible, of what he said:

> Well, my friend, you have caused a big fuss, haven't you? Not that anything's wrong with you. Personally, I'm glad you're here. But you'll have to make up your mind, if you'll excuse the expression, about what you're going to do. You just can't stand there indefinitely and make strange noises. People can't take off their clothes and not know what to do next. People will think you're crazy, or that they're crazy, and what good will that do? Get hold of yourself, make a decision, do something. If you don't, I'm going home, make supper, and forget the whole thing.

There is controversy about what happened next. This may be thought peculiar, even outrageous, considering there were a million and a half eye-witnesses near to this site — although the darkness was only lit by street lamps, a few floodlights and a three-quarters moon — but that's what happened.

Approximately half the observers now say that the huge living thing immediately began to fade as if it were a vapor, and was breathed in by the great crowd, thus disappearing. Most of the other observers adamantly now contend that the huge living thing resubmerged into the pool above the Falls, then went over them and disappeared going downstream toward the Gulf of Mexico.

The next day, the apparent mound or sandbar was gone. No radar trace of the huge living thing was found by the helicopters and boats searching the river from Minnesota to Louisiana. Photographs and films taken of the huge living thing, when developed, showed only a faint orange blur, or a white one on black-and-white film. There were no further sightings. Some experts have said the blur was caused by the unusual combination of the streetlamps, the atmosphere, and the three-quarters moon. They have suggested that the whole episode was a form of hysteria.

A group of persons who say they know about these matters, and who live in Belo Horizonte, a large city in Brazil, disagree. (The great sculptor of their region, Aleijadinho, was a man who had no hands.) Belo Horizonte is more than two hundred miles from the sea, but members of this group go every day to their center city park, and under the shadow of a famous skyscraper, they chant rhythmic songs of welcome to the huge living thing.

THE BUSINESSMAN
WHO DISAPPEARED

the businessman, as a mental exercise, deliberately notices something he hadn't observed before.

His office is also located near the city's public square and the bus terminal. Numerous beggars and drifters are usually seen in this vicinity, and the businessman passes by them every day. Over time, he has come to recognize several of them; certain ones always seem to be there. He has never once, however, given money to any of them, but he has come to know their faces. Occasionally, while riding in the elevator to the nineteenth floor of the building in which his office is located, the businessman tries to imagine what it must be like to be one of the beggars he sees every day. But he doesn't have to think about this too much because the elevator ride does not last very long. No sooner has he entered his office, he is diverted to the day's business. His secretary invariably greets him with a polite smile, and hands him the morning mail.

At four-thirty, he leaves his office, descends in the elevator, and walks to the eleven-story parking garage where his car is waiting, perhaps with a new scratch. While the attendant is bringing his car, the businessman's mood changes. After the car is parked in front of him with its motor running, the businessman walks around it, inspecting the fenders carefully. If there is a new scratch, he tersely informs the attendant of the damage, and tells him he will deduct the cost of repairing it from the current month's parking bill. The attendant always denies any responsibility for the scratch. The businessman never does deduct anything from his monthly parking bill, in spite of what he says, and this might be considered paradoxical because the businessman has often said (and probably shrewdly) that the nature of good business is deducting, in some form or another.

He usually leaves the garage at about ten minutes to five. By then, he is usually very hungry. But as he drives out to the street, he sees the beggars and drifters, and he remembers not to feel hungry again until he reaches the expressway which takes him to the small community where he lives on the outskirts of the city.

This community is not what is normally meant by a "suburb" because it was originally formed as a village by itself, and far enough from the city to have a character of its own. The suburbs at first formed a buffer between the village's isolation and the activity of the city, but the new expressway had changed that, and now many more persons live in the small community as a refuge from the city and its older suburbs.

One morning, the businessman drove to the city as he usually did, parked his car in the eleven-story parking garage, and walked to his office located near the city square and the bus station. He looked, along the way, for something new to notice, and sure enough, he saw that the painted letters on the concrete slab above the stationary store had been painted over another sign which he hadn't noticed before. Looking carefully, he could make out that the old sign had been for a meat market.

He reached the entrance of his office building. While he was in the elevator, it struck him that something had been out of place during his walk from the eleven-story parking garage to his office. But he had concentrated so much on trying to make out the old sign under the stationer's sign that it wasn't until now, while he was riding up to his office, that the uneasy sensation broke into his conscious thinking. But what was it? Then he was inside his office, and he forgot about it.

He was reminded of it that evening as he walked

to the eleven-story parking garage to retrieve his car that would take him to the expressway on which he would return to his home. Something was out of place. He could not put his mind's finger on what it was. He thought about it during the entire drive home.

The next morning he was reminded of it again as he walked to his office from the eleven-story garage. The buildings along the way seemed apparently the same. There were some new ones under construction, of course, but there was nothing unusual about them. There also seemed to be about the same number of cars in the street, the same kind of persons who normally walked past him, going to their own offices. The weather was warm and sunny — typical of the season.

But something was out of place. He was sure of it. He stopped on the sidewalk, an action he could not remember doing before so abruptly, and turned around. It was not very advantageous to stop suddenly in the middle of the sidewalk in this busy part of the city at this hour. He felt, standing there, like the broken tooth of a comb. So he moved on.

Later, sitting in his office, his mail unopened on his desk, he tried with much determination to figure out at last what was out of place on the street. At eleven-thirty, still in this determination, he got up suddenly, left his office, and departed from the building

As soon as he got to the street, he realized what it was.

Some of the beggars, some of the ones who were in the street every day, were gone. One particular man, who always wore a certain gray coat and who had peculiar eyes, had always stood on the street corner nearest the bus station holding a small dirty can. He was not now in his place. He hadn't been there yesterday, either, now that the businessman thought about it.

But he had been there every day, it seemed, for the past ten years at least, or as long as the businessman had been walking by this route to his office.

What was so unusual about this beggar's eyes was that the right one was hazel and the left one was light blue. The businessman had made that his observation one day years ago.

Another regular, the one who wore three sweaters no matter what the temperature was (and had only half a nose), he was gone, too. And the man with magenta birthmarks all over his face, he was gone. But the old man who drooled constantly and wore slippers all the time, he was in his customary location. So was the man with no legs and stringy hair, the one who moved about on a little wheeled cart. And most of the transient beggars he had noticed recently, they were on the street, too. But it was peculiar for so many of the regular beggars to be missing from the street. The businessman went back to his office, and by the time he had reached his desk, he had concluded that some of the beggars had caught the summer flu that was then going around.

It also just then occurred to him that women are rarely seen in the street as beggars. His telephone rang, however, and he became immersed in his business once again.

That evening, while he was walking to his car, he noticed that the old beggar who was always drooling, and wore slippers, was nowhere to be seen. The next morning, the businessman couldn't find the legless, red-haired beggar on his wheeled cart. By that evening, not one of the familiar beggars could be seen, and there weren't many transients and drifters visible, either.

The businessman couldn't stop thinking about this mysterious circumstance — although it was hardly germane to his business, and in no way he could imagine, connected to his personal life. When he arrived home, he didn't speak much to his wife, he forgot to scold his children, he didn't call any of his friends on the telephone and arrange to play bridge. It was very simple, he thought, I will go up to one of the beggars in the morning, and ask him what has happened to the other beggars. If he did that, of course, he would have to give the beggar something (which he had never done before out of principle) because you can't ask a beggar for information and not give him something. In this case, however, he concluded that a payment would be entirely justified because he would be receiving a service, and after all, services don't come free.

And so, the next morning he practiced the question he would ask after he parked his car in the eleven-story parking garage and was walking to his office. He hurriedly left his car with the attendant, after arriving in the city, and impatiently waited for the elevator to take him to the street. Once in the street, he immediately searched for a beggar. He didn't see any on the first block, so he made his way to his office on the second block. He was only a few yards from the entrance to his building when he realized that there were no beggars to be seen anywhere on the street. He then began walking sidestreets, streets he couldn't remember walking before, but he had no luck there. Finally, he went up to a policeman directing traffic at an intersection, and asked him what had happened to all the beggars. But the policeman hadn't noticed their absence until then, and said, why it's true, there aren't any to be seen, how strange. He promised the businessman he would ask the captain about it later in the morning when he got back to the station.

Back in his office, the businessman called the city's only daily newspaper, and inquired if the newspaper knew why all the beggars seemed to be gone. But the reporter on the telephone acted as if the businessman were a crank caller, so he hung up.

At this point, one might be expected to say that "a strange thing suddenly happened to the businessman" — except that there was no sign that anything sudden came over him at all. His actions and accompanying gestures indicated that his behavior was quite in natural sequence, and he displayed no peculiar emotions. He called his wife, who was at home, and told her that he was staying in the city for the night. He rang for his secretary and told her he was going out of town on business. He went to the washroom and removed his coat and tie. He did not rebutton the collar on his shirt. He rolled up his sleeves and took off his watch. Each thing he had taken from himself was carefully put in a half-empty large drawer in his desk. Then he walked out of his office and took the elevator to the street. He went into the hardware store on the corner and purchased a plastic folding cup. He walked over to the bus station, but he did not enter the station. A few steps to the side of the station door, he turned on his heel, opened the folding cup, and began to beg.

If he thought something would happen right away, he was wrong. Nothing happened. He just stood there. It was not unpleasant standing in front of the bus station holding a plastic cup. His mind was not busy. His body seemed only to be making internal transactions. Two persons gave him money, but they put only pennies and nickels into his cup. No one seemed to look at him, either. He didn't leave his place at lunch time; he stayed. At twelve-thirty, he saw one of his business acquaintances, an important executive, walking across the street in a furtive manner. In the middle of the block facing the bus station, the executive turned suddenly and slipped into a book store that sold magazines and films about sex. Soon after this, a woman stopped in front of him, and asked if he had eaten yet that day. When he said, No, he hadn't, she nodded, closed her kindly distant eyes, and put a dollar bill into his folding cup.

Someone he knew must have seen him begging in front of the bus station because after a few more hours, his wife drove up in her car, opened the car window, and called to him. She did not leave the car, and so the businessman who was now a beggar went over to the car. She said his name again, fiercely this time, in tones filled with pleading and anger and confusion.

Please come home now, get in the car with me, she said. Think of your children, think of me, she said. We'll get the best specialists, she said.

He told her, confused as he was for the moment, he was also somehow sure that he knew what he was doing, that he must do it, that it would be over soon, and then he would come home and everything could be all right. He said again that everything could be all right.

She drove away. The cars behind hers were now honking their horns insistingly because this side of the street was reserved for taxis only. So she drove away.

Very soon after his wife had driven off, a dark blue car drove up to the curb in front of him. Funny, he thought, I don't recognize the make or the year. The right front window came rolling down, and a young girl poked her head out of the dark blue car, and looked directly at the businessman who was now a beggar.

Come with us, she said.

The back door of the dark blue car flew open, and the businessman who was now a beggar folded his cup as he walked to the car and climbed in.

While the car drove through the city streets, the businessman realized that he felt no particular anxiety,

[44]

and at the same time, no particular anticipation. He knew that he was going where he was going.

Soon, the car was passing through the suburbs, and then through farm lands, and finally into the hills of the nearby backlands; on dirt roads, over sharp curves, rolling, rolling until they reached a small wood shack with a single, broken front window. Here we are, said the girl, and everyone got out of the car and ran inside. The girl waited for the businessman who had become a beggar, and when he walked to the small porch, she motioned to him to go in. And he did go in with her.

There was no furniture in the shack. There was a single room, completely empty. There were no other persons in the room. The man turned to the girl. She pointed to a door. He went over and opened the door. It led by a stairway to a basement. He heard the noises of others down in it. The girl was behind him as he walked down the stairs and entered the basement.

The basement did not appear to have any walls. He could not see any walls. The room seemed to extend to the horizon — although this did not make any sense. It seemed that there were thousands of young boys and girls, thousands more of young men and women, and even some small children, in the basement. And he also saw the beggars. Not as many beggars as young persons, of course, not nearly so many, but there were lots of beggars in the room.

This is ridiculous, thought the man, this is more ridiculous than a dream. And it was ridiculous in a way, whatever ridiculous is, and it wasn't a dream at all because it was actually happening.

What is happening here? the man asked the girl who had brought him to the basement. But the girl was no longer behind him, nor even in sight. The man went up to a group of four who seemed to be talking to each other. What is happening here? he asked them. They did not seem to hear him.

The man, surprising himself, screamed.

No one seemed to notice. But when he went up to another group, and touched the shoulder of one of them, he was immediately embraced gently by each of them. It seemed to be a passionless embrace. It seemed to be a kind of ritual.

What is happening here? he asked himself. Then he saw that the young persons in the basement were slowly removing the clothes the beggars wore, and were eating those clothes, most of which were rags to begin with. Someone came up to him then, and tried to rip away his shirt.

What are you doing? the man shouted at the boy. The boy paid no attention to the question, but kept on tugging at the man's shirt. The man slapped the boy. The boy smiled, laid himself down in front of the man, and pulled at his shoe.

Then a sharp drum began to beat. Its sound rose louder and louder, monotonous and insistent.

What is happening here? the man cried out to no one in particular.

He looked for the stairway, and was afraid he would not find it again. But he did find it, and he ran up the stairs into the shack. He ran immediately out of the shack to the car. The keys had been left in the car, so he started the motor and drove away, going in what he thought to be the direction of his own house.

And it was in the direction of the community where his house was located. When he got to his driveway, he saw his wife talking to their daughter in the backyard. He got out of the car, nearly numb with relief, and ran to his wife and daughter.

At first, his wife did not seem to notice him. He put his arms around her shoulders, put his lips on her lips, and pressed his body to her body. She embraced him then, surprised but without much feeling. She kept on talking to her daughter.

What is happening here? he shouted at his wife.

She did not reply. He felt something inside him, something he would have ordinarily called an abstraction, become a powerful feeling.

He grew calm. The woman said to her daughter, your father is not as he was, not at all as he was. But pretend, the woman said to her daughter, as if nothing has happened. Don't make this worse than it is, she said. The little girl began to cry. The woman's eyes filled with tears. The former businessman stood quietly near them.

It happened so gradually, he thought as he turned away, and began walking in the direction of the hills which could be faintly seen from the road.

C.1

 c.1

Hanisan, Maureen.

Secrets of successful
speaking

5/87

West Hartford Public Library
West Hartford, Conn.

A BOOK FOR:
THE BUSINESSWOMAN
THE VOLUNTEER WOMAN
THE PROFESSIONAL WOMAN
AND EVERY ASTUTE WOMAN
WHO REALIZES
THAT HER VOICE AND HER SPEECH
ARE AS IMPORTANT
AS HER WARDROBE